MORKIES, MORKIE PUPPIES, AND THE MORKIE

From Morkie Puppies to Adult Morkies
Includes: Teacup Morkie, Morkie Dog, Maltese Yorkie, Finding Morkie
Breeders, Temperament, Care, And More!

By Susanne Saben
© DYM Worldwide Publishers

DYM Worldwide Publishers

ISBN: 978-1-911355-04-5

following any of the treatments or methods highlighted in this book. Website links are for informational purposes only and should not be seen as a personal endorsement; the same applies to any products or services mentioned in this work. The reader should also be aware that although the web links included were correct at the time of writing they may become out of date in the future. Any pricing or currency exchange rate information was accurate at the date of writing but may become out of date in the future. The Author, Publisher, distributors, and/or affiliates assume no responsibility for pricing and currency exchange rates mentioned within this work.

Foreword

Dogs come in all shapes and sizes, but none are more adorable than the cuddly little Morkie dog. This designer dog breed is the result of a crossing between a purebred Yorkshire Terrier and a purebred Maltese. Each Morkie is unique, but these dogs generally exhibit the best qualities from each of the parent breeds. If you are looking for a small-breed dog that has a beautiful coat, a lively temperament, and a friendly personality, then the Morkie may just be the right breed for you.

As an experienced dog owner myself, I have to say that Morkies are one of my favorite breeds. Not only do I own one myself, but I have seen the joy that Morkie puppies and adult Morkies have brought to my friends. Whether you are looking for a companion pet to sit on the couch with you at home or a furry friend to carry with you as you run your errands, Morkies are a great option.

The Morkie breed is a great option for new and experienced dog owners alike. These dogs are very playful and good-natured, plus they love to spend time with people. As is the case for any pet, however, Morkies do require a certain degree of care in order to keep them happy and healthy. To make sure that your Morkie puppy gets the attention and the quality of care that he deserves, be sure to learn as much as you can about these dogs before you bring one home. In this book, I have compiled a wealth of information about the Morkie breed in combination with my personal experience with the breed to give you a complete and detailed care guide for these lovely little dogs.

Table of Contents

Chapter One: Introduction

Just look at that button nose! Who could say No to a dog that cute?

What do you think of then you hear the word "Morkie"? Do you picture some kind of strange creature? Perhaps something from an alien planet? While I can't blame you for thinking that way, "Morkie" is actually the name of a cuddly little dog breed - one of my absolute favorite breeds, in case you're wondering. The name comes from a combination of two different breeds – the Yorkshire Terrier and the Maltese. At one time the breed was originally known as the Yorktese but, personally, I am happy that it is now more commonly known as the Morkie, and it is one of the most popular designer dog breeds out there.

If you want to know my opinion, I think that the Morkie is one of the best dog breeds out there because they are small, friendly, and full of life – they also make great companion pets, and they do not require a great deal of exercise! Now, I don't have anything against getting a little exercise, but if your life is as busy as mine, you will be glad that your Morkie will get along just fine without a two-hour walk every day. I simply don't have time for it!

Not only are Morkies cuddly and easy to care for, but they have a personality like no other dog breed I've ever encountered. Each Morkie is different, of course, but my experience with them is that they are some of the brightest, friendliest little dogs you'll ever come across. Before you settle on purchasing a Morkie dog for yourself or your family, however, you need to learn some valuable Morkie information to ensure that you know what you are getting into with this breed.

In this book, you will find a collection of invaluable tips and tidbits about this wonderful breed. My own Morkie has brought endless light to my life, and I am confident that you will enjoy the same benefits with your own Morkie. I wouldn't be a responsible dog owner, however, if I didn't recommend that you take the time to familiarize yourself with the breed and its care requirements before you get one. That is what this book aims to provide – all of the information you need to understand the Morkie dog breed and to care for it properly.

So, what are you waiting for? Turn the page and keep reading to discover what makes the Morkie so great!

Useful Terms to Know

AKC – American Kennel Club, the largest purebred dog registry in the United States

Almond Eye – Referring to an elongated eye shape rather than a rounded shape

Apple Head – A round-shaped skull

Balance – A show term referring to all of the parts of the dog, both moving and standing, which produce a harmonious image

Beard – Long, thick hair on the dog's underjaw

Best in Show – An award given to the only undefeated dog left standing at the end of judging

Bitch – A female dog

Bite – The position of the upper and lower teeth when the dog's jaws are closed; positions include level, undershot, scissors, or overshot

Blaze – A white stripe running down the center of the face between the eyes

Board – To house, feed, and care for a dog for a fee

Breed – A domestic race of dogs having a common gene pool and characterized appearance/function

Breed Standard – A published document describing the look, movement, and behavior of the perfect specimen of a particular breed

Buff – An off-white to gold coloring

Clip – A method of trimming the coat in some breeds

Coat – The hair covering of a dog; some breeds have two coats, and outer coat and undercoat; also known as a double coat. Examples of breeds with double coats include German Shepherd, Siberian Husky, Akita, etc.

Condition – The health of the dog as shown by its skin, coat, behavior, and general appearance

Crate – A container used to house and transport dogs; also called a cage or kennel

Crossbreed (Hybrid) – A dog having a sire and dam of two different breeds; cannot be registered with the AKC

Dam (bitch) – The female parent of a dog;

Dock – To shorten the tail of a dog by surgically removing the end part of the tail.

Double Coat – Having an outer weather-resistant coat and a soft, waterproof coat for warmth; see above.

Drop Ear – An ear in which the tip of the ear folds over and hangs down; not prick or erect

Entropion – A genetic disorder resulting in the upper or lower eyelid turning in

Fancier – A person who is especially interested in a particular breed or dog sport

Fawn – A red-yellow hue of brown

Feathering – A long fringe of hair on the ears, tail, legs, or body of a dog

Groom – To brush, trim, comb or otherwise make a dog's coat neat in appearance

Heel – To command a dog to stay close by its owner's side

Hip Dysplasia – A condition characterized by the abnormal formation of the hip joint

Inbreeding – The breeding of two closely related dogs of one breed

Kennel – A building or enclosure where dogs are kept

Litter – A group of puppies born at one time

Markings – A contrasting color or pattern on a dog's coat

Mask – Dark shading on the dog's foreface

Mate – To breed a dog and a bitch

Neuter – To castrate a male dog or spay a female dog

Pads – The tough, shock-absorbent skin on the bottom of a dog's foot

Parti-Color – A coloration of a dog's coat consisting of two or more definite, well-broken colors; one of the colors must be white

Pedigree – The written record of a dog's genealogy going back three generations or more

Pied – A coloration on a dog consisting of patches of white and another color

Prick Ear – Ear that is carried erect, usually pointed at the tip of the ear

Puppy – A dog under 12 months of age

Purebred – A dog whose sire and dam belong to the same breed and who are of unmixed descent

Saddle – Colored markings in the shape of a saddle over the back; colors may vary

Shedding – The natural process whereby old hair falls off the dog's body as it is replaced by new hair growth.

Sire – The male parent of a dog

Smooth Coat – Short hair that is close-lying

Spay – The surgery to remove a female dog's ovaries, rendering her incapable of breeding

Trim – To groom a dog's coat by plucking or clipping

Undercoat – The soft, short coat typically concealed by a longer outer coat

Wean – The process through which puppies transition from subsisting on their mother's milk to eating solid food

Whelping – The act of birthing a litter of puppies

Chapter Two: Morkie Temperament and Morkie Dog Overview

Morkies love nothing more than treats and playtime with you!

Before you can truly decide whether or not the Morkie is the right breed for you, you need to learn what a Morkie is. The Morkie is known by several different names including the Yorkie Maltese and the Maltese Yorkie, among others. Morkies are small dogs, but they have a lot of energy and a lively personality. In this chapter, you will learn the basics about the Yorkie Maltese mix known as the Morkie including the history of the breed, information about its temperament, and the different types of Morkies. After reading this chapter, you'll have a better idea whether the Morkie is a good fit for you.

1.) What is a Morkie Dog?

The Morkie is not a purebred dog – it is a combination of two different breeds. The two parent breeds for this dog are the Yorkshire Terrier and the Maltese. Though the name "Morkie" is the name most commonly used for these dogs, other names have been used as well, including the following:

- Maltese Yorkie mix
- Yorkie and Maltese mix
- Maltese Yorkie
- Yorkie Maltese
- Yorktese

As a crossbreed, Morkie dogs exhibit a combination of characteristics and personality traits from the two parent breeds. Because genetics can be so complex, however, it's hard to predict which exact traits a litter of Morkie puppies will have. To give you a better idea what to expect from a Morkie adult, take a moment to learn the basics about the two parent breeds. In the following pages, you will receive an overview of the Yorkshire Terrier as well as the Maltese breeds.

a. Yorkshire Terrier Breed Overview

That long, luxurious coat sure is pretty, but it is a nightmare to groom!

The Yorkshire Terrier (also known as the Yorkie) is one of the smallest breeds of dog, often classified as a Toy breed. This breed was developed during the 19th century in a part of Northern England known as Yorkshire. These dogs were bred to catch rats in clothing mills, so they had to be small enough to fit under the machines. The average Yorkshire Terrier adult weighs no more than 7 pounds (3 kg), though there is a trend toward very small Yorkies called Teacup

Yorkies. These are simply Yorkshire Terriers that weigh under 4 pounds (1.8 kg) when they are fully grown.

While the breed's small size is one of the main defining characteristics for the Yorkshire Terrier, what really sets these dogs apart is their long, silky coat. Yorkies have long coats of silky, straight fur that is traditionally parted down the middle of the back. The fur on the back of the neck all the way down to the base of the tail is a silver-blue to dark gray color (sometimes black) and the tail itself is very dark. The fur on the head, chest, and legs is tan in color. The long coat of this breed means that regular brushing and grooming is required.

Many people say that the Yorkie is a hypoallergenic breed because it doesn't shed. This isn't entirely true – I can tell you from experience. Yorkshire Terriers do shed (all dogs do) but it is only a small amount, and they do not produce as much dander as other breeds which is what typically causes allergic reactions. So, the Yorkie is not a completely hypoallergenic breed, but it is a good choice for people who suffer from allergies.

In terms of personality and temperament, the Yorkshire Terrier is an active and curious little dog. These dogs can be very playful, and they often develop strong, protective bonds with their families. This breed can develop a bit of a stubborn streak if you aren't firm and consistent with training, but they are smart enough that standard dog training methods usually work well. These dogs do not require a great deal of exercise, but they do need plenty of mental stimulation to keep them from getting bored and developing problem behavior.

One thing you need to know about Yorkshire Terriers is that they bark – a lot. This fact makes the Yorkie a great watch dog, but it can be a little annoying to have your dog barking like crazy every time someone walks by the house. Many Yorkie owners have success in training their dogs to respond to a "Hush" command to stop barking – Yorkies can also be trained to "Speak" on command.

The Yorkshire Terrier is a friendly little dog, but it is not the right choice for everyone. These dogs can get along with older children, but they are not a good choice for families with young kids, mainly because younger children do not know how to properly handle a small dog. Yorkies are a fairly healthy breed, having an average lifespan of between 13 and 16 years, but they are prone to certain health problems like bronchitis, portosystemic shunt, cataracts, digestive problems, and reactions to anesthesia and injections.

b. Maltese Breed Overview

Like the Yorkie, the Maltese is a very small breed of dog often described as a Toy breed. These little dogs are considered an ancient breed which means that they were developed centuries ago. Maltese dogs come from the Central Mediterranean Area, and their name translates from the Latin *"Canis Melitaeus"* to "ancient dog of Malta" in English. Though it is well-known that the Maltese is an ancient breed, the exact details of its origins are unknown. It may have been developed in Asia from the now-extinct Tibetan Terrier, and it was probably crossed with various other terrier breeds as it made its way across the Middle East and into Europe.

The Maltese has a lovely coat as well, and they are darn cute when you add a bow!

The Maltese dog typically weighs no more than 8 pounds (3.6 kg) at maturity, and it stands a maximum of 10 inches (25 cm) high. These dogs are known as much for their small stature as they are for their long, silky white coats. The Maltese has a single coat of pure white fur – some specimens of the breed develop curly coats, but that is considered to be a fault for the breed. Like the Yorkshire Terrier, Maltese dogs shed a very limited amount which makes them an excellent choice for allergy sufferers. It is important to note, however, that their long coat requires lots of maintenance in the form of brushing, bathing, and trimming.

In terms of temperament, the Maltese was developed to be a companion pet. It has a lively and friendly personality, but it doesn't require a great deal of exercise, and it is an excellent choice for apartment or condo life. These dogs can sometimes be snappy around young children, but they generally do well with older children, though supervision is always recommended. This breed requires a lot of human interaction on a daily basis because it is prone to developing separation anxiety.

The Maltese is a relatively healthy breed with a long lifespan averaging 15 to 18 years. Like all dogs, however, it is prone to several health problems. Maltese dogs are prone to tear staining and eye problems like glaucoma and progressive retinal atrophy. They are also prone to dental problems, shaker dog syndrome, and a liver defect called portosystemic shunt. Responsible breeding practices can help to rule out these conditions.

2.) Maltese Yorkie Facts and Information

Bath Time!

Now that you know a little more about the Yorkshire
Terrier and the Maltese, you have a firm foundation of
knowledge on which to build your understanding of the
Morkie breed. After being introduced to the two parent
breeds, you may have a few questions about the Morkie
dog. <u>Some common questions people ask about Morkies are</u>
<u>listed here below</u>:

What are Morkie puppies like?

To give you a mental picture of what a Morkie puppy is like, imagine a tiny little bundle of fur with a stubby tail, short legs, and a lively personality. Morkie puppies are very small when they are born, and the average litter size is between 3 and 5 puppies. As is true for all dog breeds, the personality traits a Morkie puppy exhibits may be different from the traits you see in your full grown Morkie. It is important to keep this in mind when picking out puppies from Morkie breeders. As your puppy grows up, his personality might change a little bit based on the amount of socialization and training you provide. That's right – you have the power to shape your puppy to some degree based on his experiences during the first few months of life.

Is the Morkie hypoallergenic?

The Morkie has a very soft, silky coat that usually grows very long. Morkies do not have an undercoat, and they generally shed to a very small degree compared to other dogs. This being the case, the Morkie is a good choice for allergy sufferers, though it is not completely hypoallergenic (no dog that has fur is).

What is the Morkie personality like?

When it comes to Morkie temperament, you can expect your dog to be lively and curious. Both parent breeds for this Yorkie and Maltese mix are dogs bred to be companion pets so they do not require a great deal of exercise, but they are still active dogs that love to play. Because the Morkie is a cross of the Maltese and Yorkie breeds, it is difficult to predict exactly what the Morkie personality will be like. Most Morkies are very people-oriented, loving to spend time with family, and they develop strong bonds with their owners. Morkies can be a little bit yappy but with training, this kind of behavior can be controlled.

How big is a Morkie full grown?

Again, because the Morkie is a Maltese and Yorkie mix, it's hard to predict the exact size of an adult Morkie. Yorkshire Terriers typically weighs between 4 and 7 pounds (1.8 to 3 kg) at maturity, as does the Maltese. There are, however, always variations in size when it comes to dog breeding, so it is possible for a Morkie adult to be larger or smaller than either parent breed. There is also something called a Teacup Morkie which weighs a maximum around 4 pounds (1.8 kg).

What are the requirements for Morkie grooming?

Because the Morkie has a long coat, it requires a certain degree of grooming to keep it under control. Brushing your Morkie's coat several times a week will help to prevent matting and it will also help to distribute the natural oils produced by special glands in the skin which will keep your Morkie's coat shiny. Another aspect of Morkie grooming is keeping your dog's coat trimmed – you may not want to trim your dog's coat if you plan to show him but Morkies kept as pets often have their coats clipped short for convenience.

Does the Morkie have any health problems?

All dog breeds are prone to certain health problems, and the Morkie dog is no different. What you need to realize about this breed is that the health problems the Morkie exhibits can come from two different gene pools – the Yorkshire Terrier pool and the Maltese pool. Some people say that mixed breed dogs are healthier than purebreds because they have a larger gene pool to draw from. It is important to realize, however, that if both the parent breeds are prone to the same health problem, the Morkie's risk for that condition will actually be higher. You will learn more about the health problems common in Morkies later in this book but for now, you may be interested to know the most common conditions: eye problems, dental problems, portosystemic shunt, hypoglycemia, collapsed trachea and patellar luxation.

a. Summary of Yorkie Maltese Information

Given the summaries of the two parent breeds and the answers to the questions in the last section, you should have a good understanding of what the Morkie is like in general.

Below you will find a summary of some of the most relevant facts about the Morkie breed:

Pedigree: cross of Yorkshire Terrier and Maltese

AKC Group: not recognized by the AKC or The Kennel Club in the UK; recognized by the Designer Dog Registry and the International Designer Canine Registry

Types: Morkie, Teacup Morkie, Micro Teacup Morkie

Breed Size: small

Height: 6 to 8 inches (15 to 20 cm)

Weight: 4 to 7 pounds (1.8 to 3 kg)

Coat Length: long

Coat Texture: single layer; silky, smooth, straight

Color: any combination of white, tan, brown, silver, blue, or black including solid colors

Eyes and Nose: dark brown or black

Ears: erect or flopped; small and covered in fur

Tail: short and stubby

Temperament: active, playful, curious, friendly, spunky

Strangers: may be wary around strangers, make good watchdogs

Other Dogs: generally good with small dogs if properly trained and socialized

Other Pets: may get along with cats; may have a tendency to chase smaller animals

Training: intelligent and very trainable; may have a bit of a stubborn streak

Exercise Needs: very active and playful but does not require a great deal of exercise

Health Conditions: eye problems, dental problems, portosystemic shunt, hypoglycemia, collapsed trachea and patellar luxation

Lifespan: average 12 to 15 years

Litter Size: average 3 to 5 puppies

3.) *Morkie Dog History*

The practice of crossbreeding dogs is by no means new, so it is entirely possible that the Morkie breed was first created decades ago. No one kennel or Morkie breeder claims to be the original founder of the breed and because the Morkie is a hybrid it's hard to trace its exact origins. It is commonly believed that the Morkie breed originated in the United States where so-called designer dogs have become very popular in recent years.

There is a great deal of controversy surrounding the use of the term "designer dog". While some people think that the Morkie and other crossbreed dogs are superior to purebreds, others do not. Many dog owners and breeders believe that designer dogs are nothing more than mutts – a crossing of two or more distinct breeds. Whether or not you choose to play into the designer dog trend is up to you, but the fact remains that the Morkie makes an excellent companion pet.

4.) Teacup Morkie and Variations on the Maltese Yorkie Mix

As you already know, the Morkie is the result of a cross between a purebred Yorkshire Terrier and a purebred Maltese. It is important to note that Morkies can also be created by breeding two Morkies together. The amount of Yorkshire Terrier and Maltese blood that goes into the crossing affects which traits the Morkie puppies will exhibit. This is why it is difficult to make accurate predictions about Morkie puppies.

In addition to the traditional Morkie type, there are other variations and mixes of the breed that you may come across when looking for Morkie puppies. The Teacup Morkie is still a cross between a Yorkie and a Maltese, but the two parent dogs are very small specimens of the breed. Some breeders label their pocket-sized dogs Teacup Yorkies or Teacup Maltese. Breeding a teacup variety of either breed with a standard Yorkie or Maltese will produce what is known as a Morkie Teacup or Teacup Morkie.

When looking for a teacup Morkie breeder, you may also come across something called a Micro Teacup Morkie. There is no standard definition or description for this variation of the breed, but you can expect these dogs to be

very, very small. It is important to remember that the
Teacup Morkie and the Micro Teacup Morkie are not
separate breeds – they are just different sizes of the Morkie
dog breed. Do not fall prey to hobby breeders who market
their puppies as rare and sell them for exorbitant prices.
These breeders typically do not have much experience
breeding dogs, and they may not choose quality breeding
stock. When you buy from a hobby breeder (also known as
a "backyard breeder"), you have a high risk of buying a
puppy that is poorly bred and carrying any number of
inherited health problems.

Chapter Three: Morkie Dog Practical Information

Keeping watch! This Morkie is on guard against squirrels and birds.

Hopefully, by now you have a general understanding of what the Morkie breed is and what it is like as a pet. Before you can really decide whether this is the right breed for you, however, you need to learn some practical Morkie information. In this chapter, you will learn whether or not you need a license for your Morkie and you will learn about keeping Morkies with other pets. You will also receive an overview of costs such as Morkie price and a list of pros and cons for the Morkie breed. Take this information to heart when making your decision.

1.) Do You Need a License?

Before you buy any kind of new pet, you need to make sure that it is legal for you to keep that pet in your area. Licensing requirements and pet permits are different in different states and in different countries, so do not make any assumptions. Even if you are not required to license your dog by law, there are still some advantages to doing so. When you license your dog, your dog will be assigned a specific license number that will be associated with your contact information – if your dog becomes lost and someone finds him, he or she may be able to contact you using the information from the license.

In the United States, there are no federal requirements for licensing pet dogs – these requirements are determined at the state level. Most states require dog owners to obtain a dog license that is renewable annually, though there are some that do not. Dog licenses in the United States only cost about $25 (£17.35), and they must be paired with an updated rabies vaccination; each year you will have to renew the license and prove that your dog is current on his rabies vaccine as well.

In the United Kingdom, licensing requirements for dogs are a little bit different. All UK residents are required to obtain an annual license for their dogs, and the cost is similar to the expense of a dog license in the U.S. One major difference is that dogs in the U.K. do not need to be vaccinated against rabies because the virus has been eradicated. If you plan to move your dog into or out of the country, however, you will need to obtain an Animal Movement License (AML) to make sure your dog doesn't contract or spread any disease during his travels.

2.) Will a Full Grown Morkie Get Along with Other Pets?

Best friends forever! Morkies that are raised with other pets can get along just fine.

Whether or not your Morkie gets along with other pets depends on a number of different factors. For one thing, your Morkie's genetics may predispose him to chase small animals; this comes from the history of the Yorkshire Terrier and its development for hunting rats. The Maltese, however, was bred solely as a companion pet so your Morkie may or may not develop this tendency.

Another factor to consider is the socialization and training your Morkie receives. For all dogs it is a good idea to start training and socialization as early as possible – puppies are the most impressionable during the first three months of life, so that is when you want to teach them the most. You will learn more about socialization and Morkie training later in this book, but just realize that the experiences your Morkie puppy has while young will shape the way he acts as a Morkie adult.

You also need to think about what kind of other pets you have in the house. Both Yorkshire Terriers and Maltese dogs can get along with cats, especially if they are raised with them – this means that the same is likely to be true for the Morkie. Because the Morkie is such a small dog, however, he may not get along with very large or boisterous dogs. Morkies are generally good with smaller dogs, but they can be a little snappy at times around bigger dogs. You also need to supervise your Morkie's interaction with other pets just in case.

3.) *How Many Morkies Should You Get?*

The answer to the question, *"How many Morkies should I get?"* is not simple or straightforward – it depends on a number of factors. For one thing, you need to make sure that you can provide for the needs of one Morkie before you even think about getting a second. If you are sure that you are able to support two Morkies, it may be a good idea. Morkies are very people-oriented, and they require a lot of daily attention. If you work a full-time job or spend a lot of time away from home, you may want to get a second Morkie to keep your dog company. The second dog doesn't necessarily have to be a Morkie but if it is the two will be more likely to get along based on similarities in size and personality traits.

4.) *Morkie Dog Price and Costs*

As cute as they are, don't forget that dogs can be expensive!

Before you decide for sure whether or not to buy a Morkie you need to make sure that you can financially support a dog. Not only do you need to think about the Morkie price, but you also have to factor in recurring costs for food, veterinary care, and grooming expenses. In this section, you will receive an overview of the initial costs of owning a Morkie as well as the recurring monthly costs of Morkie ownership.

a. Initial Costs to Keep a Maltese and Yorkie Mix

The initial costs for keeping a Morkie (or any other dog) include the price to purchase the dog, the cost of a crate and/or dog bed, food and water bowls, toys and accessories, microchipping, vaccinations, spay/neuter surgery, and grooming supplies. You will find an overview of each of these costs as well as an estimate for each cost below:

Morkie Price – When you start thinking about where to find Morkie puppies for sale you will probably see a wide range of prices. It is important to remember that Morkies are a hybrid breed, not a pure breed, so you shouldn't pay purebred prices. The average cost for a puppy from a Morkie breeder is anywhere from $700 to $3,000 (£486-£2,082). A Teacup Morkie puppy may be on the higher end of the price range while a regular Morkie puppy may be a little cheaper. If you chose to get your dog from a Morkie Rescue, the cost of Morkies for Adoption is usually under $300 (£208).

Crate/Dog Bed – One of your biggest tasks as a dog owner is to housetrain your dog and having a crate will make this task much easier for you. Because Morkies are so small, you will only need a small crate, and you can make it more comfortable for your dog with a blanket or dog bed. The average cost for these things together is around $50 (£35).

Food/Water Bowls – Investing in quality food and water bowls for your Morkie is a good idea because he will be using them every day. The best food and water bowls to get are stainless steel because they are easy to clean – ceramic is another good option. The average costs for a quality set of stainless steel bowls are about $20 (£14).

Toys/Accessories – In addition to providing your Morkie with food and water bowls, you also need to have a selection of toys on hand to keep him busy. You should also invest in a quality dog collar and/or harness as well as a leash. You should budget about $50 (£35) for all of these costs combined.

Microchipping – Having your Morkie microchipped is not a requirement, but it is an excellent idea. A microchip is similar to a license in that it comes with a number that is correlated with your contact information. The difference is that the microchip is implanted under your dog's skin so it cannot be lost. The procedure only takes a few minutes, and it doesn't hurt your dog – plus, it only costs about $30 (£21) if you go to a clinic or shelter.

Vaccinations – When puppies are born they rely on antibodies from their mother to keep them safe from disease. Over the first year of life, your puppy will also need certain vaccinations to protect him against common canine diseases. Depending what Morkie breeder you get your puppy from, he may already have one or more vaccinations under his belt. Still, you should budget a cost of about $50 (£35) for initial vaccinations to be safe.

Spay/Neuter Surgery – One of the biggest costs you need to consider for your Morkie puppy, is spay/neuter surgery. Unless you plan to breed your Morkie (which is something you need to think carefully about before you do it), you should have your dog altered before 6 months of age. If you go to a veterinary surgeon, this procedure could cost you hundreds of dollars, but you can save money by going to a vet clinic. The average clinic cost for spay surgery is $100 to $200 (£69 - £139), and the average cost for neuter surgery is around $50 to $100 (£33 - £69).

Grooming Supplies – On top of the costs already mentioned, you will need to have certain grooming supplies on hand to keep your Morkie's long, silky coat in good condition. You should have a wide-toothed comb to work through tangles as well as a wire-pin brush for daily brushing. You may also want to invest in some dog nail clippers as well as a trimmer. The cost for these supplies varies depending on quality, but you should set aside about $50 (£35) to be safe.

To put all of this information together in your head, here is a chart detailing the costs for one Morkie and for two Morkies as well as a total cost at the end:

Initial Costs for Morkie Dogs		
Cost	**One Dog**	**Two Dogs**
Morkie Price	$300 to $3,000 (£208 - £2,082)	$600 to $6,000 (£416 - £4,164)
Crate/Bed	$50 (£35)	$100 (£69)
Food/Water Bowls	$20 (£14)	$40 (£28)
Toys/Accessories	$50 (£35)	$100 (£69)
Microchipping	$30 (£21)	$60 (£42)
Vaccinations	$50 (£35)	$100 (£69)
Spay/Neuter	$50 to $200 (£35 - £139)	$100 to $400 (£69 - £278)

Grooming Supplies	$50 (£35)	$50 (£35)
Total	$600 to $3,450	$1,150 to $6,850
	(£416 – £2,394)	(£798 – £4,754)

*Prices may vary by region and are subject to change.
**These values are calculated based on an exchange rate of $1 = £0.69

b. Monthly Costs for a Yorkie and Maltese Mix

The monthly costs for keeping a Morkie as a pet include all of the recurring costs you need to cover on a monthly or yearly basis. These costs may include the cost of food and treats, veterinary care, license renewal, grooming costs, and others. You will find an overview of each of these expenses as well as an estimate for each cost below:

Food and Treats – Because the Morkie is a small-breed dog, your monthly costs for food shouldn't be too high. You can expect to spend about $30 (£21) on a large bag of high-quality dog food that will last you about a month.

Veterinary Care – After your puppy gets his initial vaccinations and he reaches 1 year of age he will only need to go to the vet about twice a year, every six months. The average cost for a vet check-up is about $40 (£28). If you have two vet visits per year and divide that total cost over 12 months, you will get a monthly cost around $7 (£4.86).

License Renewal – Renewing your Morkie's license each year will not be a major expense – it should only cost you about $25 (£17). If you divide that cost over twelve months, you are left with a monthly cost of just $2 (£1.40).

Grooming Costs – One of the biggest recurring expenses you should budget for your Morkie is professional grooming. Even if you brush and bathe your Morkie on a regular basis, you will probably still want to have him professionally groomed and trimmed about four times per year (or more). The average cost for Morkie grooming is about $50 (£35) and four visits per year divided over twelve months is a monthly cost around $17 (£12).

Unexpected Costs – In addition to all of these monthly costs that you can predict you may find certain unexpected costs popping up once in a while. Some examples may be replacement collars or toys, cleaning supplies, special treats, etc. These costs will vary, but you should set aside about $10 (£7) each month to be prepared.

To put all of this information together in your head, here is a chart detailing the costs for one Morkie and for two Morkies as well as a total cost at the end:

Monthly Costs for Morkie Dogs		
Cost	**One Dog**	**Two Dogs**
Food and Treats	$30 (£21)	$60 (£42)
Vet Care	$7 (£4.86)	$14 (£9.70)
License Renewal	$2 (£1.40)	$4 (£2.80)
Grooming	$17 (£12)	$34 (£24)
Other Costs	$10 (£7)	$20 (£14)
Total	$66 (£46)	$132 (£92)

*Prices may vary by region and are subject to change.
**These values are calculated based on an exchange rate of $1 = £0.69

5.) *Morkie Dogs Pros and Cons*

Every dog breed is unique in its own way, and you need to consider both the pros and cons for that breed before you buy one – the Morkie dog is no different. Only if you have a thorough understanding of the breed can you really decide if it will be a good fit for you and your family. <u>Below you will find a list of advantages and disadvantages of the breed that you should consider when deciding whether this is the right breed for you</u>:

Pros for the Morkie Dog Breed

- Very small size makes a great apartment or condo dog
- Friendly and lively personality, bonds very closely with owners
- Can get along with small dogs, cats, and older children for the most part
- Very attractive breed with a long, silky coat
- Generally, responds well to training, though some develop a stubborn streak
- Very high life expectancy, between 12 and 15 years
- Tendency to bark at strangers makes a good watchdog
- Fairly low needs for exercise, not overly energetic

Cons for the Morkie Dog Breed

- Very long coat requires a good deal of Morkie grooming including brushing, bathing, and trimming
- Tendency toward barking... can be controlled with training
- May have an increased risk for certain health problems like eye conditions, dental disease, and portosystemic shunt
- Some develop a stubborn streak which can make training challenging at times
- May require a great deal of attention and interaction to prevent problem behaviors and separation anxiety
- Small size leads to fragility, especially with puppies; careful handling is required

Chapter Four: Morkie Puppies and Where to Find Morkie Puppies for Sale

Morkie puppies are more likely to sleep in your shoes than chew on them!

By now you should have a pretty good idea whether the Morkie is a good choice for you or for your family. If you think that a Morkie is a good fit, your next step is to figure out where to buy one! I would personally encourage you to consider adoption as an option but, if you have your heart set on a puppy, you should take the time to find a reputable breeder and to pick out a healthy puppy. In this chapter you will find all of the information you need to choose a

reputable breeder, to pick out a healthy puppy, or to find a
Morkie rescue dog.

1.) Where to Find Morkie Breeders

Depending where you live, you may or may not be able to find a Morkie puppy simply by walking into your local pet store. Even if your store does have Morkie puppies, however, I would encourage you to look elsewhere. Many people do not realize that a large number of pet stores get their puppies from puppy mills. A puppy mill is a breeding operation that puts profit over the welfare of the dogs. They force dogs to reproduce litter after litter with minimal veterinary care, keeping them in squalid conditions.

While a reputable Morkie breeder will be very careful about choosing breeding stock that is in good health, puppy mills don't take any precautions; they are all about profit. If the parents used for breeding purposes by the puppy mill aren't screened, there is a high risk that they will pass on congenital conditions, some of which can be very serious. Do yourself and your future puppy a favor by going through a responsible breeder to ensure that your puppy starts his life in good health.

If you are wondering where to find Morkie puppies for sale, the Internet is a good place to start. By performing an online search, you will find plenty of options for where to find Morkies for sale, just keep in mind that you should vet your

potential breeders before you pick one. You want to make
sure that the breeder isn't a puppy mill, for one thing, and
you should also make sure they are a legitimate business
and not a backyard breeder. <u>To find a reputable Morkie
breeder, follow these steps</u>:

- Ask around at pet stores, vet offices and clinics for
  recommendations of local Morkie breeders – you can
  also perform an online search.
- Compile your list of options and then view the website
  for each breeder as the first stage in your vetting
  process.
  - o Look for key information such as registration with
    a local or national breed club.
  - o Read all information provided on the website
    carefully to get clues about the breeder's
    knowledge and experience (keep in mind that not
    all reputable breeders will have a detailed website).
  - o Look for red flags like extremely high prices,
    wrong information about the breed, and general
    lack of information.
- Eliminate any breeders from your list that you can
  simply by viewing their websites and then contact the
  remaining breeders by phone or schedule a face-to-
  face interview.

- o Ask each breeder detailed questions about the
  Morkie breed to make sure they have a lot of
  experience – the breeder should also know a lot
  about the Yorkshire Terrier and the Maltese.
- o Ask the breeder about the pedigree for the puppies
  – are they bred from purebred parents or are they
  second-generation puppies? (See hybrid dog
  genetics information in Chapter 7: Morkie Dogs
  Breeding Information).
- o Ask about the breeder's policy for reserving and
  purchasing a puppy – a responsible breeder won't
  sell a puppy without meeting you.
- o Listen to see if the breeder asks you questions in
  addition to answering yours – responsible breeders
  want to make sure that their puppies go to good
  homes.
- Narrow down your list of breeders again, eliminating
  those that do not make the cut and schedule a tour of
  the breeding facilities for two or three remaining
  breeders.
  - o View the facilities where the breeding stock is kept
    in addition to seeing the puppies.
  - o Look for signs that the facilities are not kept clean –
    there should be no signs of diarrhea in the area (a
    sign of illness), and the breeding stock should be in
    good health.

- o Consider it a red flag if the breeder is unwilling to show you around – he should be willing to show you the parents as well as the puppies.
- Ask to see registration information and health certificates for the parents as well as the puppies – make sure they are good specimens of the breed.
- After narrowing down your list of options to one or two breeders, make your choice – you will find tips for picking out a puppy in the next section.

If you are looking for a teacup Morkie breeder or you want to find Maltese Yorkie puppies for sale, you can follow this same process. Just keep in mind that there may be fewer options out there for reputable breeders for Yorktese puppies (Yorkie Maltese puppies). When you are looking for where to find teacup Morkies for sale you still need to make sure that the breeder you choose is experienced and knowledgeable about the breed to ensure that the puppy you bring home is well-bred and in good health.

2.) *How to Choose a Healthy Morkie Puppy*

Morkie puppies can be quite the handful - literally!

After you have taken the time to select a reputable Morkie
breeder carefully, your job is not over! You then have to go
through the process of choosing a puppy. I know from
experience that it can be tempting to take the first puppy
that comes waddling up to you, but I would encourage you
to remain objective until you've determined that the puppy
is well-bred and in good health. <u>When you visit your
breeder of choice and actually get a chance to look at the
puppies, follow these steps</u>:

- Watch the puppies from afar for a few minutes to see how they interact with each other – they should exhibit signs of healthy activity and playfulness.
  - If the puppies seem lethargic and uninterested in playing, they could be sick.
  - If the puppies appear to be very frightened of you, they are not properly-socialized.
  - It is normal for puppies to be a little wary around strangers but they should warm up quickly and become curious about you.
- After watching the puppies for a few minutes, approach them and kneel down – wait for them to come to you.
  - Pet the puppies gently and offer them toys to see how they interact with you.
  - If you can, pick the puppies up one by one to see how they react to being handled.
  - If the puppies let you, gently flip them over onto their backs in your arms – if the puppy has a dominant personality he may struggle, but a puppy with a submissive temperament will be calm.
- Check the puppies over one by one for signs of illness or injury. Healthy puppies will exhibit the following:
  - Clear, bright eyes with no sign of discharge.
  - Clean ears – no redness, swelling, or odor.
  - No sign of diarrhea under the tail.

- o Clean, soft fur with no patches missing, even in texture.
- o No bumps or wounds on the body.
- o Healthy activity and sound movement.
- Narrow down your options to one or two puppies and ask the breeder for specific information about their health and vet records.

Once you are able to determine that the puppy is of good breeding and is in good health, you can ask about the process for putting down a deposit on the puppy. A reputable breeder will not sell a puppy before it is 8 weeks old or completely weaned, whichever comes first. The breeder should also provide you with papers certifying the puppy's pedigree and a health guarantee if the breeder offers one.

3.) *Adopt an Adult Morkie from a Morkie Rescue*

Speaking from personal experience, raising a Morkie puppy can be very challenging. Morkie puppies are very small, so you have to be very careful with them, and you also have to deal with the classic "puppy" behaviors like chewing on things, whining at all hours, and soiling in the house. If you do not feel like you are up to the challenge of raising a Morkie puppy you have another option – you can adopt a Morkie adult from a Morkie rescue.

Before you make up your mind about rescue dogs, I want to tell you some of the benefits associated with adopting Morkie adults. For one thing, when you adopt a dog from the shelter you could literally be saving a life. While there are many no-kill shelters out there, some shelters are forced to euthanize dogs that do not get adopted within a certain timeframe because they simply do not have the space to accommodate all of the dogs that come in. When you adopt a Morkie dog from a shelter, he will be forever grateful.

Another benefit of adopting Morkie adults is the fact that they are not puppies. You may think this sounds like a joke but keep in mind that most adult dogs in shelters are already housetrained, and many of them have some degree of obedience training as well. Not only do you get to skip

the process of housebreaking a puppy, but a shelter dog
may already know the basic commands!

One thing that many people do not think of as a benefit for
shelter dogs is the fact that their personalities have already
been developed. Puppies are cute and cuddly, but their
personalities can change as they mature depending on how
they are treated and how well they are socialized. The
puppy you start with could be drastically different from the
Morkie adult you end up with. When you adopt a rescue
dog, you have the opportunity to get to know the dog first
so you can determine if you are a good match.

If you think that adopting a Morkie might be a good choice,
take the time to find a local shelter in your area. You may
also be able to find Morkies for adoption at a specialized
Morkie rescue.

To help you find Morkies for adoption in your area, here
are some links to rescues and shelters that may have
Morkies available:

United States Morkie Rescues

American Maltese Association Rescue.
https://www.americanmalteserescue.org/

Northcentral Maltese Rescue, Inc.
http://malteserescue.homestead.com/

Yorkshire Terrier National Rescue.
http://www.yorkierescue.com/

Save a Yorkie Rescue. http://www.saveayorkierescue.org/

Small Paws Rescue. http://www.smallpawsrescue.org/

Small Dog Rescue, Inc. http://www.woofmanor.com/

Tiny Paws Rescue. https://tinypawsrescue.com/

United Kingdom Morkie Rescues

The Yorkshire Terrier & Toy Breed Rescue.
http://www.yorkieandtoybreedrescue.co.uk/

The Yorkshire Terrier Club of Scotland Rescue.
http://www.thekennelclub.org.uk/

The Maltese Club Welfare and Rescue.
http://www.themalteseclub.co.uk/

Small Dog Rescue. http://www.smalldogrescue.co.uk/

The Little Dog Rescue. http://www.littledogrescue.co.uk/

Chapter Five: Morkie Dog Care Guide

This little Morkie wants nothing more than to play with you!

What many people love about the Morkie breed is the fact that it is very small – this means that it can do well in smaller living spaces like urban condos and apartment buildings. Not only is the Morkie very small, but it doesn't have high needs for exercise either. In this chapter you will learn the basics about Morkie care including tips for meeting your dog's need for exercise, creating a healthy and high-quality diet, and grooming your dog's coat. Making sure that your Morkie's needs are met is your job as a dog owner, so take all of this information to heart!

1.) Morkie Full Grown Home Requirements

As you already know, Morkies only grow to an average height of 6 to 8 inches (15 to 20 cm) and a maximum weight of 4 to 7 pounds (1.8 to 3 kg). This being the case, your Morkie doesn't need a large amount of space. Still, if you want your dog to be happy in your home, you need to provide him with certain things. I personally recommend setting aside a specific area of your home that your Morkie dog can call his own.

a. Setting Up a Space for Your Morkie

Even if you do not work a full-time job, or you have a good deal of free time, there will always be times when you cannot physically keep an eye on your Morkie. In times like these, you may want to keep him confined, so he doesn't get into trouble, but you may not want to go so far as to keep him in his crate. My suggestion is to set aside a particular area in your house that your Morkie can call his own. Use a puppy playpen or something similar to block off a small space in one of the rooms of your house and then use that area to house your dog's crate as well as his food and water bowls and his toys.

Creating a space like this will ensure that you have somewhere to put your Morkie when you can't keep an eye on him, but it will still give him the freedom to move around and to play with his toys without getting into trouble. I still recommend that you keep your Morkie in his crate overnight but once your dog is housetrained you can keep him in his play area during the day when you are away from home or when you are at home but cannot keep a close eye on him.

When it comes to setting up your Morkie's play area, there are a few key things you need to include:

- Dog Crate
- Dog Bed or Blanket
- Food and Water Bowls
- Assortment of Toys

Once of the most important things you need when you bring your Morkie home is a dog crate. The ultimate goal is to teach your dog that the crate is his own personal space – you want him to feel safe there. In order to do this, you need to acclimate him to the crate by including it in your training and play times. Once you set up your Morkie's play area, be sure to incorporate the crate into your play time. Toss treats into the crate for your Morkie to chase and feed your Morkie some of his meals in the crate until he is comfortable enough that you can close the door of the crate while he is in it and he doesn't whine.

When purchasing a crate for your Morkie, the size is very important. It may seem like a good idea to purchase a big crate, so your Morkie has plenty of room, but it is actually better to buy a small crate – your Morkie will have plenty of space in his play area. The size of the crate is very important when it comes to crate training – you want the crate to be just large enough for your dog to comfortably stand up, sit down, turn around, and lie down in without an excessive amount of extra space. The goal is for your dog to view the crate as his "den" – dogs have a natural aversion to soiling their dens so this will be important come housetraining time for your dog.

In order to make the crate comfortable for your dog, you should line it with a soft blanket or dog bed. While your Morkie is undergoing crate training you may want to stick to a blanket, just in case he has an accident. Once your dog has been housetrained, you can switch to a comfier dog bed, if you like. There are many different types of dog beds to choose from, and some are specifically designed to be used in dog crates. Be sure to shop around a bit before you choose one so you know what your options are.

In addition to your dog's crate and his bed, you also need to keep his food and water bowls as well as an assortment of toys in his play area. It is up to you what type of food and water bowls you choose, but I personally recommend stainless steel. Stainless steel bowls are lightweight and easy to clean, plus they don't scratch like plastic bowls – this means they are less likely to harbor bacteria. If you don't like stainless steel, ceramic is my second choice. You may also want to invest in a plastic feeding mat – this will help to contain any spills.

In terms of toys, you want to provide your Morkie with a large assortment when he is a puppy. Give your puppy time to decide what kinds of toys he prefers and then keep several of them on hand. Having a few toys that your Morkie really likes will come in handy when you have to deal with problem behaviors like chewing. For example, when you find your Morkie chewing on a shoe or something he shouldn't have, simply tell your Morkie "No" in a firm voice and take the item away. Immediately give your dog one of his favorite chew toys and praise him when he chews on that instead – this will help to teach him what he is and is not allowed to chew on.

b. Tips for Exercising Your Dog

I have found that most Morkies are very playful and active dogs, but they do not necessarily need a great deal of daily exercise. If you have the time, your Morkie will appreciate a 30-minute walk once a day, but you may also be able to meet his needs for exercise with some active play time at home. There are plenty of games you can play with your Morkie to give him some extra exercise. Here are some examples that I like:

- Tug of war
- Fetching a ball or toy
- Hide and seek
- Red light, green light
- Jump over the stick

In addition to physical exercise, you also need to make sure that your Morkie gets some mental stimulation as well. Morkies are smart little dogs, and they are prone to developing destructive behaviors if they get bored. I personally recommend investing in a few interactive dog toys and games – Kong toys are a great option, and you can find others online. I like to leave a Kong toy or an interactive game with my Morkie when he is in his play area just to make sure he doesn't get into trouble. This is a great tactic to use if your Morkie has separation anxiety as well – give him the toy just before you leave so he is distracted and doesn't get worked up about you leaving.

c. Recommended Accessories for Morkies

In addition to your Morkie's crate, food bowls, and an assortment of toys there are a few other accessories I would recommend. The most important of these is probably your Morkie's collar and leash. Your dog's collar should be tight enough that he can't easily slip out of it but loose enough that it doesn't impact his breathing. This will probably mean that you need to buy different collars as your Morkie grows or use an adjustable collar. The size and weight of your Morkie's leash should be proportional, so you may need to start with a very short and lightweight leash for your puppy and then move to a slightly larger leash when he reaches his full size.

I would also encourage you to invest in a dog harness. Dog harnesses are highly recommended for larger dogs and for dogs that have a tendency to pull on the leash because it gives you a little more control over the dog. I am a fan of harnesses for all dogs because it helps to distribute the force from pulling on the leash across the dog's back instead of concentrating it all on his throat. Many dog owners also use head harnesses, but I find that a traditional body harness is usually enough for my Morkie.

Aside from your Morkie's collar, leash, and harness you may also want to think about some optional accessories like booties, a dog sweater, and an anti-anxiety jacket. The pads of your Morkie's feet are covered in thick skin, but in the winter you may need an extra layer of protection in the form of booties. Wearing booties can not only prevent ice from accumulating between your dog's toes, but it can also protect his feet from rock salt and chemical-laden ice melt during the winter. A dog sweater might also be necessary for the winter months, especially if you keep your Morkie's coat cut very short.

An anti-anxiety jacket is something that I personally use for my Morkie because he doesn't like loud noises, especially thunder. This type of jacket is designed to fit snugly against the dog's body, helping him to feel more secure. These jackets are available in a wide variety of sizes, and they are generally easy to use and easy to clean. This is not a necessary accessory for all dogs, but it may come in handy if your Morkie develops a fear of thunder and other particularly loud noises.

2.) Morkie Dog Feeding Guide

Yum yum yum! Morkies love to eat!

Many inexperienced dog owners mistakenly believe that choosing a dog food is as simple as walking into a pet store and grabbing a bag off the shelf. While this is certainly an option, it is generally not the best choice if you want to make sure that your Morkie gets a high-quality diet that meets his nutritional needs. Like humans, dogs require certain nutrients in specific ratios in order to be healthy. What many dog owners don't realize, however, is that those ratios are very different for dogs than they are for humans. In this section, I will tell you everything you need to know about dog nutrition and help you pick a quality dog food.

a. Nutritional Needs for Morkie Dogs

In order to remain healthy, dogs require a balance of protein, fat, and carbohydrates in their diet. They also need plenty of fresh water and certain vitamins and minerals. As you can probably guess, wild dogs are primarily carnivorous which means that most of their nutrition needs to come from animal products. Unlike cats who are obligate carnivores, however, domestic dogs are a little more omnivorous – they can derive nutrition from both animal and plant products, though animal products are infinitely more biologically valuable for dogs.

For dogs, protein is the most essential nutrient because it provides the building blocks for healthy muscles and tissue. Protein is especially important for growing puppies as well as pregnant and lactating dogs, though all dogs need a certain degree of protein in their diet to maintain lean muscle mass. Protein for dogs should come from high-quality animal sources like poultry, meat, fish, and eggs – all of these are considered "complete" protein sources. This simply means that they contain all ten amino acids that a dog's body cannot synthesize on its own. The remaining twelve amino acids are called non-essential because your dog's body can produce them. According to the Merck Veterinary Manual, the minimum protein requirement for puppies is 22% of the total diet and for adult dogs, it is 18%.

Keep in mind that these are absolute minimums – the higher the protein content, the better.

Next to protein, fat is the next most essential nutrient for dogs because it is the most highly concentrated source of energy. Per gram, protein and carbohydrates contain 4 calories each, but fat contains 9 calories per gram. Fatty acids are also important for maintaining your dog's skin and coat health, plus it plays a role in boosting his immune health as well. Like proteins, fats for dogs should come from animal-based sources like chicken fat or salmon oil. Plant-based fats like flaxseed, canola oil, and other plant oils are not necessarily bad for your dog, but they are less biologically valuable than animal-based fats. The minimum fat requirement for puppies is 8% and, for adult dogs it is 5%; again, these are minimum values.

Dogs do not have a specific requirement for carbohydrates in their diet. For wild wolves, most of the carbs they consume are found in the stomach contents of their prey. Domestic dogs, however, can benefit from low levels of carbohydrate in their diet to provide dietary fiber as well as essential vitamins and minerals. Keep in mind that the dog's body is designed primarily to digest proteins and fats – any carbohydrates in your dog's diet must be easily digestible. This means that they should come from whole grains like brown rice and oatmeal or grain-free options like potatoes, peas, sweet potatoes, and tapioca. These carbohydrates should also be cooked to make sure that your dog's body can digest them.

In terms of how much your dog needs to eat, his calorie requirements will vary depending on his age, size, and activity level. Morkie puppies need a lot of calories to sustain healthy growth and development. Even once your Morkie reaches his adult size, however, he will still need a more calorie-dense diet than a dog two or three times his size. Small-breed dogs like Morkies have very fast metabolisms which mean high-calorie needs; they also generally need more fat in their diets than large-breed dogs. Protein is still the most essential nutrient, however.

Think about this – an Akita that weighs 110 pounds (50 kg) needs a daily calorie intake around 2,500. Your 5.5-pound (2.5 kg) Morkie, on the other hand, only needs about 250 calories. If you do the math, however, you will find that the Akita needs about 23 calories per pound of bodyweight while the Morkie needs about 45 calories per pound of bodyweight. One of the best ways to make sure your Morkie's calorie needs are met is to feed him a high-quality dog food formulated for small-breed dogs. These dog food formulas are rich in protein, and they are also higher in fat than large-breed formulas. You may also need to feed your Morkie more frequently than you would feed a larger dog to keep his metabolism going strong.

b. Choosing a Healthy Dog Food

Now that you understand the basic nutritional needs for your Morkie you have a foundation of knowledge on which to base your understanding of commercial dog food products. Like I said earlier, you can't just go into a pet store and pick the first bag off the shelf and expect it to be a high-quality diet. Choosing a healthy dog food takes some time, and it is not a decision you should rush. The quality of your Morkie's diet will have a direct impact on his health and well-being so take this choice seriously!

When you look at a bag of dog food, you may be overwhelmed by the sheer volume of information it presents. Now multiply that by ten or twenty different brands and dozens of the various formulas at any given pet store and you may start to feel the pressure of choosing the right product. You will be glad to know, however, that deciphering all of that information on the dog food label isn't as complicated as it seems – you really only have to look at three key things.

The first thing you need to look for on the product is an AAFCO statement of nutritional adequacy. The American Association of Feed Control Officials (AAFCO) is responsible for regulating what goes into pet food and animal feed – they are also responsible for testing commercial pet food products to determine whether they meet the basic nutritional requirements of the animal for which the product was designed. AAFCO has created nutritional profiles for puppies and adult dogs, and they compare each commercial dog food product to that profile to see if they line up.

If a dog food product meets the nutritional requirements for dogs in the intended life stage – puppy (growth) or adult (maintenance) – the label will carry some kind of statement that looks something like this:

"[Product Name] is formulated to meet the nutritional levels established by the AAFCO Dog Food nutrient profiles for [Life Stage]."

In the United Kingdom, pet food regulation is based on the Feeding Stuffs Act – all ingredients used in pet food must be fit for human consumption. All products that are fit for daily consumption must be labeled "Complete Feedingstuff" or "Complete Petfood" while foods designed for intermittent feeding are labeled "Complementary Feedingstuff" or "Complementary Petfood".

When you see these things on a pet food label, you will know that, at the very least, it will meet the minimum nutritional requirements for your Morkie. You still need to delve a little deeper, however, to determine the quality of that nutrition. The next place you need to look, then, is the guaranteed analysis. This is the part of the dog food label that tells you the amount of crude protein, crude fat, crude fiber, and moisture in the product. Compare those values (presented as a percentage) to the minimum values I gave you in the last section. Remember, you want the protein values to be high, the fat values to be moderate, and the fiber values to be low. The moisture level for most commercial dry dog foods is between 78% and 82%.

After you have determined that the guaranteed analysis on the dog food label checks out, your last stop is the ingredients list. For dog foods (like people foods), these lists are presented in descending order by volume; this means that the ingredients at the top of the list are found in the highest quantity. As you can probably guess, the top of the list is where you want to see at least one source of high-quality animal protein. This can come in the form of fresh meat or meat meal. Fresh meats contain up to 80% moisture, but meat meals have already been cooked down to 10% moisture – this makes them a much more highly concentrated source of protein than fresh meats and, therefore, a very high-quality ingredient.

In addition to high-quality animal proteins, you also want to see digestible carbohydrates and animal fats near the top of the list. Be wary of any product that displays a carbohydrate source first as well as any that lists more than three or four carbohydrates; your dogs need for dietary fiber is very limited, too much carbohydrate can cause digestive issues. Remember that animal fats are more valuable than plant fats, though plant fats are not inherently dangerous.

Not only should you check the ingredients at the top of the list, but you also want to look at the end of the list – this is where you will find things like probiotics and nutritional supplements. Dried fermentation products are a very common inclusion in high-quality dog foods and they play the role of a probiotic. Chelated minerals (like copper amino acid chelate) are minerals that have been chemically bonded to protein molecules – this makes them easier for your dog's body to digest and absorb.

In addition to looking for the ingredients that ARE included on the list, you also need to pay attention to what is NOT there. Corn, soy, and wheat products offer very limited nutritional value to dogs, and they are common food allergens, so they are best avoided. You also want to make sure that the product doesn't contain any artificial colors, flavors, dyes, or preservatives. Avoid foods that are loaded with chemicals (things with names you can't pronounce or easily identify) as well as those that seem to be loaded with by-products or unnamed protein sources (you want chicken meal, not poultry meal).

c. **Tips for Feeding Morkies**

By following the tips and information in the last section, you should have no trouble picking out a high-quality commercial dog food diet for your Morkie. It might take you some time to get the hang of reading a dog food label, but eventually, you will come to see that it is not as complicated as you once thought. When it comes to feeding your Morkie, choose a formula that is designed for small-breed dogs and follow the feeding recommendations on the package. Keep in mind that these are recommendations – you'll need to keep an eye on your dog's weight and activity level to see if you require to make any changes. If your Morkie starts to gain too much weight, cut back a little – if he slows down or loses weight, up it a little.

I personally recommended taking your Morkie's total daily portion and dividing it into three meals – one in the morning, one at midday, and one in the evening. This will help to ensure that your Morkie gets a steady stream of energy to support his fast metabolism. If you feed your Morkie treats, just be sure that they are very small and that they do not comprise more than 10% of his total daily intake. You should also avoid feeding your Morkie table scraps because they are high in calories, and they won't provide your dog with the nutrition he needs. If you are concerned about your Morkie's weight or diet, contact your veterinarian for a check-up.

d. Dangerous Foods to Avoid

Not only do you need to know what kind of foods are good for your Morkie, but you should also familiarize yourself with a list of foods that can be dangerous or toxic for your dog. If your dog eats any of the following, contact the Pet Poison Control hotline right away at (888) 426-4435.

- Alcohol
- Apple seeds
- Avocado
- Cherry pits
- Chocolate
- Coffee
- Garlic
- Grapes/raisins
- Hops
- Macadamia nuts
- Mold
- Mushrooms
- Mustard seeds
- Onions/leeks
- Peach pits
- Potato leaves/stems
- Rhubarb leaves
- Tea
- Tomato leaves/stems
- Walnuts
- Xylitol

- Yeast dough

3.) *Morkie Grooming Requirements*

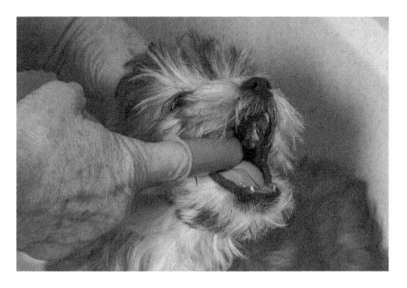

Open up! Keeping your Morkie's teeth clean is very important!

Because the Morkie is a cross between a Maltese and a Yorkshire Terrier, you should expect to perform a good bit of maintenance on his coat. Both of the parent breeds have very long coats, so your Morkie's coat will probably grow long as well. The actual texture of the coat may vary between the fine, silky texture of the Yorkshire Terrier's coat or the slightly thicker but still silky fur of the Maltese. Generally, the Morkie is a low-shedding breed, but you still need to do some work to keep his coat in good condition. In this section, you will learn the requirements for grooming your Morkie and for keeping his ears, teeth, and nails properly maintained.

a. Brushing and Bathing Your Morkie

As you already know, the length and texture of your Morkie's coat may vary depending on breeding, but you can expect it to grow fairly long and thick. Morkies have a high tendency to develop mats in their fur, so it is absolutely essential that you brush and comb your dog's coat on a daily basis. Not only can mats be unsightly on your dog, but they can irritate your Morkie's skin and may actually become very painful if they are not treated properly. If a mat gets too large, you may have to cut it out, and that can impact the appearance of your dog's coat.

On a daily basis, you should brush your Morkie's coat with a wire pin brush. The bristles should be fairly long so they can reach all the way through your dog's coat. Some Morkie owners also like to use a small slicker brush to help remove dead hairs from the dog's undercoat. When you brush your dog's coat, start at the back of his head and work the brush slowly down the back of his neck and along his body. Always brush in the direction of hair growth and move slowly just in case you encounter a mat.

If you come across a mat while grooming your Morkie, try using a wide-toothed comb to carefully work through it. Do not pull on the mat – just use the teeth of the comb to separate the hairs a few at a time. If you are absolutely not able to work through the mat, you can cut it out with a pair of small, sharp scissors. To do so, pinch the hair at the base of the mat between the mat and your dog's skin (so you don't accidentally cut your dog). Use the scissors to cut through the mat a few hairs at a time, gently pulling on the mat until it starts to come free.

After your Maltese has been thoroughly brushed, you can then bathe him. Simply fill your bathtub with a few inches of lukewarm water then wet down your dog's coat using a cup or a hand sprayer. Squeeze a tiny bit of dog-friendly shampoo into your hand then work it into your dog's coat until it is thick and lathered. Thoroughly rinse your Morkie's coat to remove all traces of soap, being careful not to get any water in your dog's ears or eyes. Use a damp washcloth to clean your dog's face then towel him dry. If it is very cold, you may want to blow-dry your dog using the lowest heat setting.

In addition to brushing and bathing your Morkie on a regular basis, you should also have him professionally groomed every 6 to 8 weeks. You may be able to learn how to trim your dog's coat yourself, but the results will be more even if you let a professional do it. It is up to you whether you leave your Morkie's coat long or cut it short – it just depends on how much maintenance you are willing to do. Personally, I give my Morkie a puppy cut – this involves trimming all the hair to a length of 1 to 2 inches (2.5 to 5 cm) all over the body. This cut is very manageable, and it looks absolutely adorable too.

b. Cleaning Your Morkie's Ears

Because the Morkie has drop ears (ears that hang down on either side of the head), these dogs have a higher risk for ear infections than other breeds. If your dog's ears get wet, they may not get enough air circulation to dry them out before bacteria starts to grow, and that can lead to an infection. This is why it is so important to keep your Morkie's ears dry during a bath. You should also clean your Morkie's ears about once a week just to be safe.

Cleaning your dog's ears is fairly easy – all you need is some dog-friendly ear cleaning solution and a few cotton balls. Squeeze a few drops of the solution into your dog's ear and then massage the base of the ear to distribute the solution. Then, just use the cotton balls to wipe away any debris as well as any extra solution. That's all it takes to clean your Morkie's ears! Believe me, taking a few minutes each week to do this will save you a lot of hassle in the long run and your Morkie will be glad not to have ear infections.

c. Brushing Your Dog's Teeth

The idea of brushing your Morkie's teeth may sound silly to you, but it is actually very important. Dental disease is incredibly common in dogs, and it can lead to some very serious health problems. It is important to start brushing your Morkie's teeth while he is very young so he gets used to that kind of handling. You can start by just touching his lips and teeth with your hand and then work your way up to using a toothbrush once your dog gets used to it. I am personally a fan of the rubber finger brush that you simply slip over your index finger and then use to brush your dog's teeth. Don't forget to use dog-friendly toothpaste – it comes in different flavors that your dog will like.

d. Clipping Your Morkie's Nails

Another important grooming task you need to tackle every week is clipping your Morkie's nails. If you take your dog on walks outside on the pavement, his nails will be naturally filed down to some degree, but you should still check them once a week. When trimming your dog's nails, you should only trim off the sharp tip – do not cut too much at once! Your dog's nails contain something called a quick which is the blood vessel that supplies blood to the nail. If you cut your dog's nails too short you could sever the quick and that will cause your dog pain, and it will bleed excessively.

Before you start trimming your dog's nails, have your vet or a professional groomer show you how to do it. There are plenty of products on the market that make trimming a dog's nails easy, but I am personally a fan of a simple pair of dog nail clippers. When clipping your Morkie's nails, you should also keep some styptic powder on hand, just in case. If you happen to cut the nail too short, just dip it in the styptic powder to immediately stop the bleeding. You should then keep an eye on the nail over the next few days just to make sure it heals properly.

Chapter Six: Morkie Dog Training Guide

Sit! Stay! Start early with Morkie training!

Aside from providing for your Morkie's basic needs, your most important task as a dog owner is training. Morkies are smart little dogs, so they generally take to training fairly easily, but it will still require some time and effort on your part. In this chapter, I will provide you with an overview of some of the most common training methods as well as my personal recommendation for the training method I choose. I will also walk you through the steps to crate train your Morkie – if you are firm and consistent, it should only take a few weeks.

1.) Overview of Dog Training Methods

When it comes to dog training, there are a variety of different methods to choose from and several different ways to distinguish these methods. I find it easiest to separate the dog training methods into two groups – reward-based and punishment-based. Reward-based dog training involves rewarding your dog for good behavior and punishment-based training involves disciplining him for bad behavior. Both of these methods can be used to encourage the repetition of desired behaviors and to decrease the frequency of undesired behavior.

Even if you are a new dog owner, you are probably familiar with Cesar Milan, otherwise known as the Dog Whisperer. Milan follows a particular philosophy of dog training typically referred to as Alpha Dog training. This method hinges on the idea that domestic dogs are descended from wild wolves and that they still follow a pack mentality. Milan suggests that it is your job as the dog owner to become the pack leader, and you must teach your dog to be submissive to you. With this type of training, you discipline your dog for undesirable behaviors, and you do everything in a way that establishes you as the alpha – this means that you never let your dog eat before you or go through the door before you do.

Another type of dog training involves punishment or discipline. With this type of training, you discipline your dog when he performs an undesired behavior; the discipline, or punishment, is intended to reduce the likelihood of your dog repeating that behavior in the future. For the most part, this training method is only effective in reducing undesired behaviors like chewing, barking, or digging – it doesn't really work for obedience training or house training.

One of the most popular training methods is called positive reinforcement training. With this training method, you reward your dog for performing the desired behavior – the reward acts as motivation to encourage your dog to repeat that behavior in the future. Using the reward as encouragement, you can teach your dog to associate a particular action with a command or hand signal. Many dogs have a natural desire to please their owners, and the reward adds to that motivation.

In addition to traditional positive reinforcement training, there is a variety called clicker training. This type of training utilizes the same principles of reward-based motivation, but it pairs it with a clicker device. The purpose of the device is to help the dog identify the desired behavior more quickly. To use clicker training, you simply give your dog the command and wait or lead him to perform the desired behavior. As soon as he does, you click the clicker and then immediately issue the reward. It should only take a few repetitions for your dog to form an association between the command and the behavior – at this point, you discontinue use of the clicker but keep the reward until your dog has the command down pat.

2.) Best Training Method for Morkies

Don't let them charm you with their innocent expression - Morkies need training and discipline!

Every dog owner has their own preference for dog training methods, but I personally am a fan of positive reinforcement training. Not only is positive reinforcement one of the most effective training methods, in my opinion, but it also helps to encourage a positive relationship between the dog owner and the dog. The last thing you want is for your dog to learn to fear you – that is the risk you take with Alpha Dog training or punishment-based training methods. I find that when I use positive reinforcement training, it encourages my dog to listen to me, and he is more likely to come when I call him because he likes being near me.

a. Choosing the Right Motivation

The key to positive reinforcement training is to find something that will motivate your dog to perform the desired behavior. In most cases, a combination of food rewards and verbal praise is effective. You also need to make sure that you choose the best word to use as your command – Sit is easier for your dog to learn than Sit Down. You want to keep your commands short and sweet – you also need to make sure that they are easy to distinguish from one another. Once you choose a command for a particular behavior, stick to it and ensure that everyone in your household uses the same one.

When it comes to choosing the food reward for positive reinforcement training you need to choose wisely. While you are training your Morkie, you may do as many as three training sessions per day, each with multiple repetitions for several different commands – that adds up to a lot of food rewards. This being the case, you want to choose treats that are very small but loaded with flavor, so they motivate your dog properly. You can also hold one or two of your dog's training sessions at meal times so you can use pieces of his kibble as food rewards. You should also make sure only to use food rewards every time until your dog gets the hang of the command; then, you can start to phase them out.

b. Sample Training Sequence

Not only is positive reinforcement training a highly effective training method, but it is also very easy to use. The key to this type of training is to choose a simple command, to teach your dog the behavior that is associated with the command, and to reward him for performing that behavior. Following this simple training sequence, you can teach your Morkie to do just about anything. <u>Here is an example of the training sequence to teach your dog to sit</u>:

1. Kneel down in front of your Morkie and pinch a small treat between the thumb and forefinger of your dominant hand.

2. Get your Morkie's attention with the treat by waving it in front of his nose.

3. Hold the treat just in front of your Morkie's nose and tell him to "Sit" in a firm and clear tone.

4. Immediately move the treat up and forward toward the back of your dog's head.

5. Your Morkie should lift his nose to follow the treat and, in doing so, his bottom will lower to the floor.

6. As soon as your dog's bottom hits the floor, tell him "Good dog" and give him the treat.

7. Repeat this training sequence several times until your Morkie responds consistently with the appropriate behavior.

8. Continue practicing with your Morkie, slowly reducing the frequency of food rewards but remaining consistent with verbal praise.

Once your Morkie has this training sequence down you can modify it for other basic commands like Down, Stay, and Come. The key is to guide your dog to perform the desired behavior and to immediately praise and reward him when he complies, so he learns to associate the command with the desired action. This is where a clicker comes in handy if you are interested in trying clicker training.

3.) Morkie Puppy Crate Training Guide

You may have heard that small-breed dogs are notoriously difficult to housetrain. This may be the case for some dogs, but if you follow this crate training guide, you should be able to housetrain your Morkie in just a few weeks. Remember, the key to crate training is to remain firm and consistent both in your commands and with your rewards. When you reward your dog for performing a certain behavior, he is more likely to repeat it in the future.

Here is the training sequence I personally recommended for crate training a Morkie:

1. Choose a specific area of the yard where you want your Morkie to do his business – you can fence off a small area or simply choose a particular corner.

2. Take your Morkie outside every hour or two and lead him directly to this chosen location.

3. Tell your Morkie "Go pee" (or choose another simple command) as soon as he gets to that particular area.

4. Wait for your Morkie to do his business – if he does, immediately praise him in a very excited voice and

give him a small treat.

5. If your Morkie doesn't have to go, immediately take him back inside instead of letting him wander.

6. Keep a close eye on your Morkie at all times when he is in the house – try to confine him to whatever room you are in so you can watch him.

7. Watch your Morkie for signs that he has to go and take him outside immediately if he starts to sniff the ground, walk in circles, or squat – this is in addition to taking him out every hour or two.

8. When you cannot physically watch your Morkie, keep him confined to his crate to reduce the risk of him having an accident – do not keep any food or water in the crate with him.

9. Limit your Morkie's time in the crate to just a few hours until he is old enough to hold his bladder and bowels for a longer period of time.

10. Always let your Morkie outside immediately before putting him in the crate and after releasing him – you should also take him out after a meal or after a nap.

Be consistent about giving your Morkie plenty of chances to do his business outside and reward him for doing so – keep this up for a few weeks and he will be crate trained! Remember, puppies under six months of age can only be trusted to hold their bladders for 3 to 4 hours at a time, though they may be able to do so longer overnight. If you can't let your puppy out often enough during the day, you will need to hire a pet sitter or have a neighbor check in on your Morkie while you are gone.

Chapter Seven: Morkie Dogs Breeding

As cute as they are, Morkie puppies are a lot to handle!
Think carefully before breeding.

There is nothing better than a litter of squirming little Morkie puppies. Just because they are cute, however, doesn't mean that breeding your dog is a good idea. Dog breeding is a much more complex process than many people realize and there is some very real risk involved for the female dog. If you are thinking about breeding your Morkie to make extra money, don't! The only reason you should be breeding dogs is to preserve or improve the breed. If your motivation is monetary, your priorities are in the wrong place.

1.) General Morkie Dog Breeding Information

Before getting into the details of how dog breeding works, I want to tell you a little bit about genetics for crossbreed dogs. As you already know, the Morkie is a combination of the Maltese and the Yorkshire Terrier. But is this the only combination that will result in a litter of Morkie puppies? No! There are a number of different combinations that can be used to create the Morkie breed and I will tell you about them right now.

a. Genetics of Hybrid Dogs

When you breed a purebred to a purebred (a purebred is 100% genetically pure) you get a hybrid – the first generation of such a crossing is labeled F1. If you breed two F1 hybrids together, you get a litter of hybrid puppies which are labeled F2, or second generation. Crossing two F2 hybrids together will also result in a litter of hybrid puppies which will be labeled F3, or third generation.

These are the most basic crossings that can be done to create a hybrid like the Morkie, but they are not the only options. There is also a common breeding practice called backcrossing – this is when you breed a first generation (F1) hybrid back to a purebred dog. In the case of the Morkie, this would involve breeding an F1 Morkie with either a purebred Maltese or a purebred Yorkshire Terrier. The resulting litter would exhibit a higher degree of similarity to the purebred parent and would be labeled F1b. You can also breed an F1 hybrid to an F1b backcross dog to create a second-generation backcrossed dog (F2b).

b. Basic Dog Breeding Information

Now that you understand a little more about the genetics involved in creating hybrid dogs like the Morkie you are ready to learn the basics about dog breeding. Because both the Maltese and the Yorkshire Terrier are small-breed dogs, the Morkie is as well – this means that they may reach their adult size much sooner than a larger breed. It is important to wait, however, until your female Morkie has gone through at least two full heat cycles before you breed her, and you should not wait any longer than 5 years.

The term "heat" is generally used to describe the estrus cycle in female dogs. Once the dog becomes sexually mature, she will go into heat twice a year on average, about every 6 months. Some small-breed dogs go into heat more frequently, and it generally takes a few years for the cycle to become regular. The estrus cycle is simply the process through which the dog's body becomes fertile and ready for breeding. At some point during the cycle the ovaries release mature eggs and, if the female is mated to an intact male dog, they will become fertilized, and pregnancy occurs.

The average length of the heat cycle in dogs is between 2 and 4 weeks. For Yorkshire Terriers, the average length is about 21 days (3 weeks) and, for Maltese dogs, it is about the same – this means that you can expect your Morkie's cycle to last an average of 3 weeks in most cases. When your dog goes into heat, there will be some obvious signs such as the following:

- Swelling of the external vulva
- Bloody discharge from the vaginal area
- Increased frequency of urination, urine marking behavior
- Vocalization, whining or howling

The first sign of heat is usually swelling of the vulva, though some dogs develop a discharge first. The thickness and color of the discharge will change over the course of the dog's cycle. It may be very red and bloody at first but will become watery and pinkish in color by the 7th to 10th day of the cycle. This point in the cycle is when the dog is most fertile, and it is also when she is most receptive to the advances of the male dog. Mating your Morkie during this period will give you the highest chance of a successful conception, though sperm can live for as long as 7 days in the female's reproductive tract so she can become pregnant even days after mating.

Once the dog becomes pregnant she enters what is known as the gestation period – this is the period during which the fertilized eggs develop into fetuses in the uterus. For most dogs, the gestation period lasts between 61 and 65 days (about 9 weeks), though the average is 63. At the end of the gestation period, the puppies will be whelped (born) and the mother will care for them until they are old enough to become independent. The average litter size for the Yorkshire Terrier breed is 3 to 5 and the litter size for Maltese dogs is 2 to 4. Given this information, you can expect your Morkie to have between 2 and 5 puppies. Keep in mind, however, that first litters for dogs tend to be fairly small, usually 1 to 3.

c. Risk and Precautions to Take

Breeding dogs is not something that should be taken lightly. I have already mentioned the fact that there are some very real risks involved for the female dog, both during pregnancy and during the birth. If you do not plan to breed your Morkie, you should have him neutered or her spayed before the dog reaches 6 months of age. Having your dog spayed or neutered before 6 months will significantly reduce the chance for serious diseases like uterine infections, testicular cancer, breast cancer, and other types of cancer. In male dogs, neutering may also reduce the risk for problem behaviors like urine marking.

If you do decide to breed your Morkie you need to be absolutely sure that she is in good health and that she won't pass any inherited diseases on to her puppies. You need to have your dog tested for disease, and you should run a DNA test as well – if she is a carrier for congenital conditions, you should seriously consider not breeding her. You should definitely not breed her with a male that is also a carrier for the same diseases.

Before breeding your Morkie, have her examined by a vet to make sure she is big enough and mature enough to carry a litter of puppies to term. Feed her a healthy, nutritious diet to condition her for breeding and make sure she gets the veterinary care she needs during pregnancy. You won't have to change her diet drastically during the pregnancy, but you should be prepared to feed her a little bit more in the final stages to help her support her own body as well as the development of the puppies.

2.) *Raising Morkie Puppies Information*

Cuddle time! Morkie puppies love to snuggle.

If you are serious about breeding your Morkie, you need to start keeping track of her cycles. Do not breed your Morkie before she has completed at least 2 heat cycles but do not wait too long – the older she gets, the higher her risk for complications. You should never breed a Morkie after 5 years of age. If your Morkie isn't old enough or large enough to support a litter of puppies she may have to have a cesarean section instead of a natural birth and that comes with its own list of potential risks and complications.

Once your Morkie becomes pregnant, the puppies will grow and develop inside her for up to 65 days (the average is 63). Near the end of the gestation period, you will start to notice signs of impending labor. To make sure that your dog has a safe place to deliver her puppies, provide her with a nesting box somewhere around the eight-week mark. Place the box in a safe, quiet area and line it with old towels or blankets that you do not mind throwing out after the birth – they will get messy.

As your Morkie approaches her due date she will begin to spend more and more time in the whelping box. Do not disturb her, but keep a close eye on her to make sure that the birth goes well. If you want to get a better idea when she will give birth, start taking her internal temperature within a few days of the due date. The average internal temperature for a dog is between 100°F to 102°F (37.7°C to 38.8°C). Once it drops to about 98°F (36.6°C), labor is likely to begin within the hour. You will know that labor is starting when your dog begins to show obvious signs of discomfort like pacing, panting, and changing positions.

Once your Morkie begins to give birth, stay nearby just in case but let her do it on her own. During the early stages of labor, contractions will be about 10 minutes apart. If your dog has contractions for more than 2 hours without giving birth, take her immediately to the vet. Once your Morkie starts giving birth, she will whelp one puppy approximately every thirty minutes. After each puppy is born, she will tear open the birth sac, bite through the umbilical cord, and clean the puppy. Licking the puppy not only helps to clean it off, but it also helps to stimulate the puppy to start breathing on his own.

After all of the puppies have been born the dog should expel the afterbirth – do not be surprised if she eats it, she needs plenty of nutrition at this point. The puppies should begin nursing within an hour of being born. This is incredibly important – the first milk the mother produces is called colostrum and it is full of nutrients and antibodies from the mother's immune system. The puppies will rely on these antibodies for protection until their own immune systems develop. If your puppies do not start nursing within an hour or so, you may need to feed them by hand.

Morkie puppies are very small when they are first born – they are also blind, deaf, and completely helpless. Your puppies will rely on their mother for warmth and for food – she will also lick them to help them urinate and defecate until they are able to do so on their own. Keep an eye on the mother and the puppies but try not to interrupt them while they are nursing. You can, however, start to handle the puppies carefully, so they get used to being around people from a very young age.

By the time your puppies reach three weeks of age, their nervous system really starts to develop – this is when their eyes and ears open, plus they will start to become more aware of their surroundings. You should start offering the puppies small amounts of solid food softened with water or broth around 5 weeks of age. The puppies will still be nursing, but they may start to sample the food. By the time the puppies reach 8 weeks of age, they should be fully weaned onto solid food. If they are, this is about the time that you can separate them from the mother. This is also the best time to really start focusing on socialization because puppies are the most impressionable during the first 3 months of life.

Chapter Eight: Morkie Dog Health Guide

Help your Morkie live a long, healthy life by providing him with quality veterinary care.

As you hopefully know by now, the best thing you can do to keep your Morkie healthy is to feed him a high-quality diet that meets all of his nutritional needs. Even if your dog gets a healthy diet, however, he may still be at risk for certain health problems. To keep your dog protected it is your job to familiarize yourself with the most common conditions known to affect the Morkie breed so you can identify the symptoms when they occur and then seek proper treatment from your veterinarian. You will find this information and more in this chapter.

1.) Common Health Problems for Morkies

Because the Morkie is a crossbreed, the conditions to which he may be prone could vary depending on breeding. The Morkie breed itself is not prone to any specific conditions – rather, its common health problems are determined by those known to affect the parent breeds, the Yorkshire Terrier and the Maltese. Some dog owners believe that crossbreed dogs are healthier than purebred dogs because they have a larger gene pool. This may be true in some cases, but if both parent breeds are carriers for a particular disease, then your Morkie's risk will be much higher.

In this section, you will find an overview of some of the health conditions that may affect your Morkie as determined by the health problems linked to the two parent breeds. The more you know about these conditions in terms of the signs and symptoms, the sooner you will be able to get a diagnosis and start treatment. Some of the conditions that may affect Morkies include the following:

- Collapsed Trachea
- Dental Problems
- Eye Problems
- Hypoglycemia
- Kidney Failure
- Patellar Luxation

- Portosystemic Shunt
- Tear Staining

In the following pages, you will receive an overview of each of these conditions including their clinical signs and symptoms, methods of diagnosis, treatment options, and prognosis information.

a. Collapsed Trachea

As you may already know, the trachea is another name for the windpipe, and it is the part of the throat made up of cartilaginous rings. Dog breeds like the Morkie sometimes have a problem where those rings begin to collapse which leads to an obstructed airway – this condition is called collapsed trachea. In most cases of collapsed trachea, the airway is only partially blocked. As a result of the obstruction, your dog might make honking noises, or he may start coughing. Many dogs suffering from tracheal collapse exhibit reduced exercise intolerance as well as general difficulties with breathing. You may also notice blue or pale gums due to lack of oxygen.

The exact cause of this condition is unknown, but it is generally considered to be a genetic abnormality that the dog can inherit from one or both of its parents. Morkies that have tracheal collapse are more likely to exhibit symptoms during periods of excitement, after eating or drinking, and after bouts of intense exercise. In terms of treatment for collapsed trachea, your vet might prescribe corticosteroids or cough suppressants. If your dog is obese or overweight, losing weight might help to reduce the severity of the condition. If no improvements are made within a few weeks of treatment, surgical repair may be required.

b. Dental Problems

It is a well-known fact that most dogs develop some degree of gum disease by the time they reach three years old. Not only is gum disease (also known as periodontal disease) very common in dogs, but it can be very serious as well. Unfortunately, most dogs don't show any signs or symptoms of gum disease until it is in the advanced stages. As the disease gets worse, your Morkie may experience painful chewing, gum loss, even tooth loss or bone damage. When this happens, the only treatment option available is to remove the affected teeth.

Brushing your Morkie's teeth on a regular basis is incredibly important, and it is the only way to prevent gum disease. When your dog eats, he starts to salivate, and that saliva (as well as bacteria and food particles) accumulate on the surfaces of his teeth – this film is called plaque. Over time, if the plaque is not removed it will harden into a substance known as tartar or calculus. This substance can then spread under the gums and into the root of the tooth as well as into the bone. Eventually, the bacteria may even make its way into the dog's bloodstream, causing a severe infection.

Some of the most common signs of advanced gum disease include red or bleeding gums, loose teeth, bad breath, difficulty chewing, and ropey saliva. Brushing your dog's teeth is the best way to prevent this disease, but you should also have your dog checked out by a veterinarian once or twice a year as well. Your vet will be able to take x-rays to determine the extent of the damage, and he can anesthetize your dog to perform a thorough dental cleaning if it becomes necessary.

c. Eye Problems

Small-breed dogs like the Morkie are very prone to developing eye problems, especially congenital issues like cataracts, glaucoma, and progressive retinal atrophy. Glaucoma is a condition that occurs when the fluid inside the dog's eye builds up, creating too much intraocular pressure – this leads to internal damage of the eye. If glaucoma isn't treated promptly, it can lead to a partial loss of vision or total blindness for the dog.

There are two types of glaucoma in dogs – primary and secondary. Primary glaucoma is typically genetic, determined by specific physical or physiological traits that increase the dog's risk of developing the condition. Secondary glaucoma is secondary to another condition or some kind of injury to the eye that leads to inflammation and fluid accumulation. Treatment options for glaucoma include topical solutions to reduce pressure and increase drainage as well as analgesics to relieve pain.

A cataract is simply an opacity in the lens of the eye that can lead to an obstruction of normal vision. This condition is generally not painful for the dog unless the cataract luxates, or slips out of position and floats around the eye. Cataracts are usually the result of trauma or old age, though they can be inherited when they appear in younger dogs – this condition is called juvenile cataracts. There is no way to prevent cataracts from forming, but any loss of vision may be corrected by surgery, in some cases.

Progressive retinal atrophy (PRA) is a degenerative condition affecting the retina, or the part of the eye that sees light and sends signals to the dog's brain which interprets the light as vision. Most Morkies that have PRA start to show symptoms as early as 2 months, and many of them go blind by 1 year of age. Fortunately, most dogs adapt well to the loss of vision, but you will need to help your dog out around the house. There is no cure for progressive retinal atrophy, and it is often an inherited condition – this is why responsible breeding practices are essential.

d. Hypoglycemia

More commonly known as low blood sugar, hypoglycemia is a condition that has been linked to diabetes in some dog breeds. When your dog eats food, his body breaks it down into its most basic component – glucose. The body then produces and releases insulin which helps to regulate the absorption of glucose into the bloodstream. If the dog is unable to produce or utilize insulin effectively, it could lead to chronic low blood sugar or hypoglycemia. Some of the most common symptoms of low blood sugar in dogs include loss of appetite, weakness, restlessness, vision problems, heart palpitations, and seizures.

Though there are several potential causes for hypoglycemia, it is generally a secondary condition related to diabetes. Dogs with diabetes may need to be given insulin shots to help regulate their blood sugar levels. In some cases, simply giving the dog some food when he shows signs of low blood sugar can be enough to stop the symptoms. Your veterinarian will be able to determine the best course of treatment for your Morkie.

e. Kidney Failure

Also known as renal disease, kidney failure is a condition that is sometimes seen in Yorkshire Terries which means that it could affect your Morkie – it is especially common in older dogs. Some of the potential causes of kidney failure in dogs include old age, infections, parasites, cancer, inflammation, autoimmune disease, trauma, toxicity, and certain inherited disorders. There are also many different signs of kidney disease including increased water consumption and urination, blood in the urine, decreased appetite, vomiting, weight loss, diarrhea, lethargy, and poor coat condition.

In order to diagnose your Morkie with kidney failure, your vet will have to perform several blood tests as well as a blood urea nitrogen test and a urinalysis. In cases where symptoms develop suddenly, acute kidney disease is usually to blame, and prompt treatment is required. Some potential treatments for kidney failure in dogs include fluid therapy to rehydrate the dog, changes to the diet to improve overall health, and antibiotics or other medications to treat an underlying infection. In some cases, it may even be necessary to perform kidney dialysis.

f. Patellar Luxation

It is not uncommon for small-breed dogs like the Morkie to develop musculoskeletal issues like patellar luxation. Patellar luxation occurs when the dog's patella (kneecap) slides out of its normal position in the groove of the femur, or thigh bone. During the early stages of the disease, dogs generally don't display any symptoms except while the patella is out of place and immediately after. While the patella is out of place the dog may not be able to walk normally and, once it pops back into place, the dog may show signs of soreness or tenderness.

As the condition progresses, the femoral groove may become increasingly worn down, and the patella may start to pop out of place more often. In many cases, this leads to wear and tear on the bone and joint as well as osteoarthritis and the associated pain. In severe cases, the dog may become completely lame in the affected joint. Medical treatments for this condition are rarely effective except to manage pain, but surgery often provides long-term relief.

g. Portosystemic Shunt

Sometimes called PSS, the portosystemic shunt is an inherited condition that affects the portal vein which transports blood from the circulatory system to the liver where it is filtered. Portosystemic shunt happens when there is an abnormality between the portal vein and another vein which causes blood flow to bypass the liver entirely. This means that toxins and other harmful substances aren't filtered out of the blood, and it can lead to some serious problems like stunted growth, changes in behavior, poor muscle development, and even seizures.

In many cases, dogs with portosystemic shunt don't show any symptoms until later in life. Diagnosing the disease can be tricky, and it usually involves blood tests, urinalysis, and a bile acid test. Dietary changes and certain medications are commonly prescribed for the treatment of portosystemic shunt, and they can be effective in producing rapid improvements. When these measures are not enough, surgery can help to repair the defect. The average survival rate for dogs that have surgery for this condition is over 95% which is very good.

h. Tear Staining

In Morkies, tear staining is not specifically a health problem, but it can be a symptom of some kind of eye problem. Many dogs with white or light colored fur develop stains in the corners of the eye that are usually the result of excessive tearing or irritation of the eyes. Tear stains can also be the result of blocked tear ducts, allergies, physical deformities, or even ear infections. It is possible for food allergies to cause tear staining in some dogs.

Tear staining is not painful for the dog, though the underlying cause of the staining could be. You should have your dog checked out by a veterinarian to determine the root cause of the problem, and then you can clean your dog's face using one of several methods. You can soak a cotton ball in the sterile saline solution and use it to clean away the stain – keeping the fur around the eyes trimmed short may also help to reduce irritation. Some Morkie owners also find that adding a teaspoon of organic apple cider vinegar to their dog's water helps.

Keep in mind that these are just a few of the most common conditions known to affect the Morkie breed. To ensure that your dog stays in good health you should have him checked out by a veterinarian at least once but ideally twice a year – every six months or so.

2.) Morkie Dog Vaccinations and Precautions

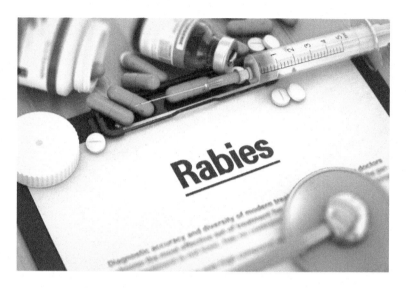

Ouch! Don't forget about your Morkie's vaccinations!

In addition to familiarizing yourself with some of the most common health conditions known to affect the Morkie breed, you should also make sure that your dog stays up to date on veterinary check-ups and vaccinations. Vaccines are designed to protect your dog against certain deadly and contagious diseases like distemper, rabies (except in the UK), and parvovirus. When your puppy is very young he will need a number of different vaccines at specific times – your vet will be able to tell you which ones he needs and when. After he gets all of his puppy vaccines, he will then need certain booster shots on an annual basis – some vaccines come in 3- or 5-year versions as well.

<u>To help you understand which vaccines your Morkie is likely to need and when consult this vaccination schedule for dogs</u>:

<u>Vaccination Schedule for Dogs**</u>			
Vaccine	**Doses**	**Age**	**Booster**
Rabies (US only)	1	12 weeks	annual
Distemper	3	6-16 weeks	3 years
Parvovirus	3	6-16 weeks	3 years
Adenovirus	3	6-16 weeks	3 years
Parainfluenza	3	6 weeks, 12-14 weeks	3 years
Bordetella	1	6 weeks	annual
Lyme Disease	2	9, 13-14 weeks	annual
Leptospirosis	2	12 and 16 weeks	annual
Canine Influenza	2	6-8, 8-12 weeks	annual

Chapter Nine: Morkie Dog Showing Guide

Look how lovely! This dog is just begging for a medal.

As a dog owner, one of the most challenging yet rewarding things you can do with your dog is participate in dog shows. In the United States, the Westminster Kennel Club dog show is the largest annual dog show – in the U.K., it is the Crufts dog show. Unfortunately, both of these shows are only open to purebred dogs so you may not be able to show your Morkie there. There are, however, several dog shows open to mixed breeds and designer dogs. In this chapter, you will learn what those shows are, and you will receive tips for showing your Morkie as well.

1.) *Show Options for Mixed Breeds*

Any experienced dog owner who trains their dogs for show will tell you that the Westminster Kennel Club dog show is the pinnacle of competition in the United States and that Crufts fills the same niche in the U.K. These shows provide dog owners around the globe with an opportunity to compete against other dogs for the coveted title of Best in Show. Unfortunately, these shows only allow purebred dogs to register for their conformation competitions.

In judging conformation shows, judges compare the dogs present to the breed standard published by the governing body, assigning points in accordance with how well the dog meets the standard. Both the Kennel Club and the AKC have established standards for all of their registered breeds. Because the Morkie is a mixed breed, however, it is not accepted by either of these breed organizations and is, therefore, ineligible for show in conformation competitions.

Before you become too disappointed, keep in mind that though the Morkie cannot participate in conformation competition at AKC or Kennel Club shows, there are other options! These shows have different structures and requirements than standard dog shows, but they can still be a great opportunity for you to bond with your Morkie. Below you will find an overview of some of the mixed

breed dog show options that may be available to you and
your Morkie:

a. Mixed Breed Dog Clubs of America

The Mixed Breed Dog Clubs of America (MBDCA) is a
national registry that accepts mixed breeds, and it offers
many of the same benefits and opportunities to those dogs
that the AKC offers to purebreds. The MBDCA offers a
number of competitions throughout the year including
rally, obedience, conformation, retriever instinct, lure
coursing, and versatility. Like the AKC, the MBDCA has
strict rules and regulations for each of their competitions
which you can find on their website. You can also find a
schedule of upcoming events on the website:

http://mbdca.tripod.com/

b. AKC Shows for Mixed Breeds

Because the Morkie is not accepted by the AKC, it is
ineligible for conformation competition. However, the AKC
does offer some options for mixed breed dogs through their
AKC Canine Partners organization. Through this
organization, mixed breeds like the Morkie can still
compete at AKC events to earn titles for various dog sports
including coursing, tracking, obedience, rally, and agility.

You can register your Morkie online and find more information about AKC dog shows through the AKC Canine Partners website:

http://www.akc.org/dog-owners/canine-partners/

c. Kennel Club Shows for Mixed Breeds

Similar to the AKC, the U.K. Kennel Club does not accept the Morkie as a breed, so it, therefore, cannot participate in conformation competition at the annual Crufts dog show. In 2000, however, The Kennel Club launched a new annual event called Scruffts which is similar to the Crufts competition but designed specifically for mixed breed dogs. In this competition, dogs have the opportunity to compete for titles like "Most Handsome Dog," "Prettiest Bitch," "Child's Best Friend," and "Golden Oldie." You can find more information about the show on the Crufts website:

http://www.crufts.org.uk/

In addition to these dog shows, there are other canine events that mixed breeds like the Morkie may be eligible to participate in. For example, dogs of any breed are allowed to register for competitions sponsored by the Canine Freestyle Federation or for disc dog competitions held by the International Disc Dog Handlers Association. Other organizations that hold mixed breed-friendly events include the North American Dog Agility Council, the North American Flyball Association, the United Kennel Club, and the United States Dog Agility Association. You can find a list of crossbreed-friendly events and organizations by using the following link:

http://www.dogchannel.com/dog-activities/dog-competition/article_8002.aspx

2.) Tips for Showing Morkie Dogs

This puppy is too young to show, but it's never too early to start practicing!

Just because mixed breed dogs can't participate in the same shows as purebred dogs doesn't mean that the competition is easy. Mixed breed dogs have the capacity to display a wide variety of skillsets based on breeding which can actually make the competition fiercer. The rules and regulations for each dog show are different, so be sure to do your research before registering your Morkie to make sure that he meets all of the requirements.

Though the exact rules and regulations may vary, here are a few basic requirements that your Morkie should meet before you start thinking about enrolling him in a competition:

- Your Morkie should be at least 1-year-old – some shows (like Scruffts) have competition classes for younger dogs, but not all will.
- Ensure that your Morkie has been completely housetrained and is able to hold his bladder for at least 6 hours.
- Make sure that your dog is properly socialized and has basic obedience training – he needs to listen to your commands, and he should be capable of remaining calm in a busy show setting.
- Your Morkie should be a good example of the breed for conformation competitions – see the show regulations to determine what that standard is.
- Ensure that your Morkie is completely up to date on vaccinations – you don't want him to contract or spread some kind of disease at the show.
- Make sure that your Morkie is clean and well-groomed – pay close attention to any requirements the show might have in regard to presentation.

As long as your dog meets these basic requirements, you should be in good shape. Be sure to go over the specific requirements for the show in great detail to make sure your Morkie complies and to ensure that you know everything you need to know about the competition. In addition to making sure that your dog meets the requirements, there are some things you should plan to bring with you to the show. Here is a good list to start with:

- Your registration information for the show
- Your dog's identification including license number and rabies vaccination info (US only)
- A grooming table and any necessary grooming supplies or equipment (for conformation)
- A dog crate and/or exercise pen
- Food, water, and treats for the entire day (for both you and your dog)
- Bowls for your dog's food and water
- Toys to keep your dog occupied
- Any medications your dog may need
- A change of clothes, just in case
- Paper towels, plastic gloves, and trash bags for after-show cleanup

In addition to being physically prepared for the dog show, you should also make some mental preparations. When you first start out in the show circuit you should be realistic – do not expect your dog to win right off the bat. It can take time to get a handle on how dog shows work and your Morkie will need to get used to it as well. Take advantage of the opportunities you have at these shows to network with other dog owners. Not only can you make new friends but you can pick up tips from people who are more experienced than you. The more you learn, the greater your Morkie's chances are of winning!

Chapter Ten: Morkie Dog Care Sheet

What's cuter than a Morkie puppy? A Morkie puppy in a basket!

By now I hope that you have an excellent understanding of the Morkie breed including its personality, temperament, care requirements, grooming needs, and more. With all of this information in mind, you have what you need to decide whether or not the Morkie is the right dog breed for you. If it is, you will be glad to have this book on hand as you do your part to be the best Morkie owner you can be. There may come a time when you have questions, or you want to reference a certain bit of information. Rather than flipping through the whole book, you will find all of the relevant Morkie information and facts in this care sheet.

1.) Morkie Information Overview

Pedigree: cross of Yorkshire Terrier and Maltese

AKC Group: not recognized by the AKC; recognized by the Designer Dog Registry and the International Designer Canine Registry

Types: Morkie, Teacup Morkie, Micro Teacup Morkie

Breed Size: small

Height: 6 to 8 inches (15 to 20 cm)

Weight: 4 to 7 pounds (1.8 to 3 kg)

Coat Length: long

Coat Texture: single layer; silky, smooth, straight

Color: any combination of white, tan, brown, silver, blue, or black including solid colors

Eyes and Nose: dark brown or black

Ears: erect or flopped; small and covered in fur

Tail: short and stubby

Temperament: active, playful, curious, friendly, spunky

Strangers: may be wary around strangers, make good watchdogs

Other Dogs: generally good with small dogs if properly trained and socialized

Other Pets: may get along with cats; may have a tendency to chase smaller animals

Training: intelligent and very trainable; may have a bit of a stubborn streak

Exercise Needs: very active and playful but does not require a great deal of exercise

Health Conditions: eye problems, dental problems, portosystemic shunt, hypoglycemia, collapsed trachea and patellar luxation

Lifespan: average 12 to 15 years

Litter Size: average 3 to 5 puppies

2.) Morkies Habitat Information Overview

Recommended Accessories: crate, dog bed, food/water dishes, toys, collar, leash, harness

Collar and Harness: sized by weight

Energy Level: fairly active

Exercise Requirements: 30-minute walk daily; may be substituted with active playtime at home

Exercise Ideas: play games to give your dog extra exercise during the day; train your dog for various dog sports

Crate: highly recommended

Crate Size: just large enough for dog to lie down and turn around comfortably

Crate Extras: lined with blanket or plush pet bed

Food/Water: stainless steel or ceramic bowls, clean daily

Toys: start with an assortment, see what the dog likes; include some mentally stimulating toys

Grooming Supplies: wire pin brush, small slicker brush, metal wide-tooth comb, small sharp scissors

Grooming Frequency: brush daily; professional grooming every 6 to 8 weeks

3.) Morkie Nutritional Information Overview

Nutritional Needs: water, protein, fats, carbohydrate, vitamins, minerals

Nutrient Values (puppy): minimum 22% protein, minimum 8% fat, low carbohydrate

Nutrient Values (adult): minimum 18% protein, 5% fat

Calorie Needs: varies by age, weight, and activity level

Amount to Feed (puppy): feed freely but consult recommendations on the package

Amount to Feed (adult): follow recommendations on the package; calculated by weight

Feeding Frequency: daily portion divided among three meals – morning, midday, evening

Feeding Tips: monitor dog's weight and activity; increase ration if low energy or weight loss, reduce ration if too much weight is gained

Important Minerals: calcium, phosphorus, potassium, magnesium, iron, copper and manganese

Important Vitamins: Vitamin A, Vitamin A, Vitamin B-12, Vitamin D, Vitamin C

Look For: AAFCO statement of nutritional adequacy; guaranteed analysis; quality ingredients at top of ingredients list;

Quality Ingredients: fresh animal protein (poultry, meat, fish, eggs), digestible carbohydrates (brown rice, oats, barley), animal fats (chicken fat, salmon oil, etc.)

Beneficial Supplements: prebiotics, probiotics, chelated minerals, vitamin supplements

Ingredients to Avoid: artificial flavors, dyes, preservatives; corn, soy, wheat ingredients; by-products and by-product meals; low-quality fillers

4.) Morkies Breeding Information Overview

Age of First Heat: around 6 months (or earlier)

Heat (Estrus) Cycle: 14 to 21 days

Frequency: twice a year, every 6 to 7 months; some small breeds have 3 cycles per year

Greatest Fertility: 7 to 10 days into the cycle

Gestation Period: average 63 days

Pregnancy Detection: possible after 21 days, best to wait 28 days before exam

Feeding Pregnant Dogs: maintain normal diet until week 5 or 6 then slightly increase rations

Signs of Labor: body temperature drops below normal 100° to 102°F (37.7° to 38.8°C), may be as low as 98°F (36.6°C); dog begins nesting in a dark, quiet place

Contractions: period of 10 minutes in waves of 3 to 5 followed by a period of rest

Whelping: puppies are born in 1/2 hour increments following 10 to 30 minutes of forceful straining

Puppies: born with eyes and ears closed; eyes open at 3 weeks, teeth develop at 10 weeks

Litter Size: average 3 to 5 puppies; first litter may be smaller, 1 to 3 puppies

Weaning: start offering puppy food soaked in water at 5 to 6 weeks; fully weaned by 8 weeks

Socialization: start as early as possible to prevent puppies from being nervous as an adult

Conclusion

Hopefully, by now you have come to see why I believe that the Morkie is one of the dog breeds out there. These cute and cuddly little bundles of love are full of personality and life – what more could you ask for in a dog? If you are thinking about getting a Morkie for yourself, I congratulate you! Getting my own Morkie was one of the best decisions I ever made and I know that you will feel the same.

Before you go out and buy your own Morkie puppy, however, I want to give you one more piece of advice. Make sure that you have the time and the energy to give your Morkie the life he deserves. It breaks my heart to see Morkie puppies abandoned in animal shelters because their owners simply didn't have the time to care for them. A dog is not just a pet; he will become your devoted friend and companion, so it is your job to make sure that you give him everything he needs. If you have any doubts that you will be able to care for your dog for the duration of his entire life, I hope you will make the responsible choice and choose another pet.

In writing this book, it was my goal to share my love for Morkies with the world and, in doing so, help others come to see the beauty of these little dogs! If you are convinced that a Morkie is the right pet for you and your family, then I wish you the best of luck – you will be very happy together!

Index

C

D

E

F

G

H

P

R

S

T

U

CPSIA information can be obtained
at www.ICGtesting.com
Printed in the USA
BVOW05s0825020117
472343BV00023B/100/P